CONTENTS

KT-163-272

What's a vlog?

A friendly face appears on your screen and starts to tell you about her day. She talks about a film she's seen or a tasty lunch she's just eaten. A week later, the same person talks about her experience at a local shop. Is this a news show? Not really. It's a video blog! Video blogs (or vlogs) are videos people make of themselves to share thoughts, opinions and experiences with viewers.

dabble lab

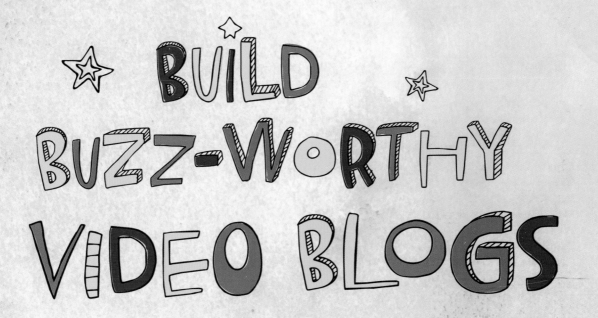

BUILD BUZZ-WORTHY VIDEO BLOGS

Thomas Kingsley Troupe

Raintree is an imprint of Capstone Global Library Limited, a company incorporated in England and Wales having its registered office at 264 Banbury Road, Oxford, OX2 7DY – Registered company number: 6695582

www.raintree.co.uk
myorders@raintree.co.uk

Edited by Shelly Lyons
Designed by Sarah Bennett
Original illustrations © Capstone Global Library Limited 2020
Picture research by Morgan Walters
Production by Katy LaVigne
Originated by Capstone Global Library Ltd
Printed and bound in India

978 1 4747 8739 0 (hardback)
978 1 4747 6799 6 (paperback)

British Library Cataloguing in Publication Data
A full catalogue record for this book is available from the British Library.

Acknowledgements
We would like to thank the following for permission to reproduce photographs: iStockphoto: mustafagull, 10; Shutterstock: Artazum, top 21, Astarina, (action) Cover, Becris, (film) design element, Birdman Music, Audio file, Carla Nichiata, bottom 21, clickyusho.id, (clock) design element, Darcraft, (rec) Cover, Dmytro Zinkevych, 4, 5, glenda, left 13, Halfpoint, 12, katarina_1, (card) design element, Keep Calm and Vector, (sticker) design element, Lapina, (boys) Cover, top 13, Lightspring, background 45, Natasha Pankina, (icons) Cover, design element, ONYXprj, (laptop) Cover, Cover, design element throughout, photolinc, (watercolor) design element throughout, Redcollegiya, (cupcake) design element, Ryan DeBerardinis, top right 31, Seth Gallmeyer, (notebook) design element, Shorena Tedliashvili, (film strip) design element throughout, silm, (sketch notebook) design element, Vissay, (poster) bottom 45, Vyacheslav Sakhatsky, (camera) design element, weikwang, (muffine wrapper) design element

Every effort has been made to contact copyright holders of material reproduced in this book. Any omissions will be rectified in subsequent printings if notice is given to the publisher.

All the internet addresses (URLs) given in this book were valid at the time of going to press. However, due to the dynamic nature of the internet, some addresses may have changed, or sites may have changed or ceased to exist since publication. While the author and publisher regret any inconvenience this may cause readers, no responsibility for any such changes can be accepted by either the author or the publisher.

Video blog success guide

Keep it simple Don't overdo it with visual effects or strange, random noises. Your content should be exciting and interesting enough to hold the attention of your viewers without having to resort to cringe-worthy antics.

Take your time Don't be afraid to reshoot pieces of video if you don't like something. If you plan to share your video with the world, you need to make sure it's right!

Be yourself A lot of YouTube or video blog "celebrities" try to put on a performance or act like someone they're not to generate followers. Break from the pack by being yourself! Acting too over-the-top and copying someone else's style is a recipe for disaster.

What you'll need

☆ an idea
☆ an outline
☆ talent/you/guests
☆ a video camera/smartphone/tablet
☆ a location
☆ lights
☆ a tripod
☆ editing software

Finding gear

Video blogging shouldn't cost you a lot of money. You can probably find what you need from around your own house. Of course, many famous video bloggers use expensive equipment, but that doesn't mean you need to. What really matters is coming up with interesting content.

Camera ready

Digital camera

One of the most important elements in making your video blog will be the camera. Find a digital camera that is simple to use and able to record long shots of video. You'll be taking lots of shots of yourself and your surroundings, so make sure the camera's memory card has space on it.

Smartphones and tablets

If you can use a smartphone or tablet as your camera, you're in luck. Not only are smartphones small and easy to use, many of them have built-in video-editing apps. If yours doesn't, you can always add one. Ask an adult to help you download the app you need. As with a digital camera, make sure there's enough memory available for all the footage you plan to shoot.

Webcam

Do you have a laptop or a personal computer? Chances are, it comes with a webcam already built in. While it's trickier to place the camera where you need it, you'll be able to see yourself as you're recording. If your computer doesn't have a webcam, you can find an inexpensive one quite easily.

Action/GoPro cameras

Using an action camera is another option. These are great for filming video blogs on the go. They're sturdy and small enough to attach almost anywhere. Make sure you use one that is able to record sound. Some of them are video only.

Lights

Light! Use a lot of it. Your viewers need to see you or whatever it is you're trying to show them. If you use too little light, your image will look grainy.

Use overhead lights, lamps or even natural light from a window. Take some sample shots and then review the footage to see what you think. If it's too bright, remove one light.

PRO TIP

Don't shoot video of yourself with your back to a bright, open window. You'll end up looking like a shadow, and people won't be able to see your face. Instead, turn and face the window and use that natural light.

Tripods

Are you planning to mainly sit and talk to the camera during your video blog? Use a tripod. A tripod will keep your camera in place and leave your hands free. You can easily find one that will work well for very little cost.

Don't feel as though you HAVE to use a tripod, though. If you're shooting your video blog on the go, you can always go "handheld". Just make sure you keep yourself, or whatever you're filming, as steady as possible. You don't want the shots to be too shaky.

phone tripod →

PRO TIP

Don't have a tripod? Use heavy objects like books to keep your camera secure and locked into place.

Ideas

The most difficult part of creating your own video blog is coming up with a good idea. Content is what the focus of your vlog is all about. What do you want to talk about? What would your viewers like to see? Ask friends and classmates what sort of videos they like to watch.

While there are no rules about what your video blog needs to be, it's good to find something you're passionate about. Do you like talking about films? Vlog about them! Are you a big fan of video games? Talk about the game you're playing. Review it for your vlog!

I love dogs!
I'm going to make a video blog on caring for dogs.

Welcome to "Awesome Eats" with Jake and Travis.

I'm going to teach sports tips in my vlog!

PRO TIP

Be careful not to say things that could be hurtful to others. And don't refer to people by name, unless you have their permission. Keep the focus on YOU and your likes and interests.

Planning makes perfect!

Schedule

A lot of popular online video bloggers (YouTubers) make frequent videos. They let their audience or followers know when they can expect to see something new from them. Some will even post a new video a few times a week.

What's your video blogging plan? Does your idea sound like it could be an ongoing thing? If so, plan out a handful of ideas and topics for future videos.

PRO TIP

You can lure in people to watch your next video by giving them a taste or "tease" of what you'll be doing next!

SUNDAY	MONDAY
31 BRAINSTORM Topics for the month	**1** Create outline
7	**8** Create outline
14	**15** Create outline
21	**22** Create outline
28	**29**

TUESDAY	WEDNESDAY	THURSDAY	FRIDAY	SATURDAY
2 Prepare for shooting	3 Shooting day!	4 Edit video	5 Reshoot and edit video	6 Post video
9 Prepare for shooting	10 Shooting day!	11 Edit video	12 Reshoot and edit video	13 Post video
16 Prepare for shooting	17 Shooting day!	18 Edit video	19 Reshoot and edit video	20 Post video
23 Prepare for shooting	24 Shooting day!	25 Edit video	26 Reshoot and edit video	27 Post video
30	1	2	3	4

Outline

Scripts aren't really necessary for video blogs. But having an outline of what you want to talk about will make your video shoots go more smoothly. You can list out all of the things you want to say or show during the course of the video.

An outline will also help you keep your thoughts together so you don't miss an important point. The last thing you want to do is have the camera rolling and not know what to do!

OUTLINE for the SHOOT

1. Introduction

2. Guest interview on tips for icing a cake
   a) Cut to the recipe when the guest mentions it.

3. Show tools and ingredients.

4. Icing the cupcakes

5. Adding bling to the icing

6. Closing

1. introduction
2. Gest interview on frosting tips
a. cut to recipe when guest mentions
3. it show tools and ingredients
4. Frosting the cupcakes
5. Adding bling to the frosting
6. Closing

PRO TIP

Instead of writing your outline on a piece of paper, put it on a mini whiteboard near the camera. This way, you can see what's next, without looking down at a script or checklist.

Crew

Making a video blog is usually a solo adventure. There may be times, however, when it'll be helpful to have a crew assist you with shooting the video. Ask your friends if they'd like to be a part of taking your video blog to the next level.

Members of your crew can do a number of different things. If you're blogging while walking, a friend could follow you with the camera. This will keep your hands free, letting you concentrate on what you're saying. Another friend can act as director to explain what should happen and where to put the camera.

PRO TIP

Getting help from a crew is great! Make sure you thank them by having water and snacks available for them during the shoot. Also, don't forget to include them in the credits for the vlog.

Backgrounds or locations

Would you want to watch someone talk into the camera while sitting in front of the same boring wall day after day? Neither does your audience! A great background or location is a requirement for shooting your video.

PRO TIP

Try to find a space where you can control the light. This will make your videos look consistent if you shoot there again.

Pick a place that's interesting to look at. Perhaps near a fireplace or a colourful bookshelf. Does your room have fun things in it? Shoot it in there. Just make sure you have permission to use the location you choose. If you choose a location that's not near by, ask an adult to take you there.

Being on camera

One of the hardest parts about video blogs is putting yourself in front of the camera. What if I look silly? Will people think I sound funny? Don't worry! If you've got interesting things to talk about, you'll be fine.

A lot of video bloggers use strange voices or create a funny act to get a lot of attention. While it might be funny at first, it can get old quickly. Practise what you're going to say a few times and get ready for the spotlight!

Today we're making my magical-rainbow-unicorn-sparkle-cupcake icing!

PRO TIP

Consider having a guest on your video blog from time to time. Sometimes, great content can be created by having someone to talk to. Anything you can do to keep your video interesting will keep viewers hooked.

Vlogging with a guest (or two) can be lots of fun! ☺ ☺ ☺

Practice shoots

Do a practice shoot of your video in advance. Don't worry about making it perfect, but try filming yourself to test it out. Pretend you're doing the real thing and record a few minutes with just you talking to the camera.

When you're filming, it can be easy to get tongue-twisted. 😛

Practising helps!

Watch the video and see if you have any nervous tics. Are you saying "uhh", "err" or any other words a lot? Are you talking too quickly? Too slowly? Are you clearing your throat too often? Watching yourself is hard, but it can help you improve your presentation.

And . . . let's try that again. Take two!

PRO TIP

Relax! The best thing you can do is be yourself on camera. Once you calm down and practise a few times, the nervousness should disappear.

Set it up

You've got your vlog outline ready. You have a good spot to shoot. You feel great about your topic and how you'll look on camera. You're even wearing your favourite t-shirt. It's time to set up your video shoot.

Position your camera and tripod so you're in the middle of the shot, with the lens just above your eyeline, but pointed down a bit. You'll want to be about an arm's length away from the camera. If possible, ask someone to help you line up your shot. When you're ready, lock the tripod and don't let the camera move.

PRO TIP

Try a few practice shots. You definitely don't want to shoot the whole video only to discover the top of your head was cut off! ☺

And ... action!

At long last, you're ready to start filming! Hit record and start talking. Use your vlog outline to help keep you on track. Do your best to look into the camera lens so it will appear you're talking directly to your viewers. Most important? Have fun!

Did you make a mistake or lose track of where you were? Don't worry! Go back to where you were and pick it up again. The great thing about video is that you can shoot a lot of footage. Even better, you can fix mistakes when you're editing.

PRO TIP

Resist the urge to play back every chunk of video you shoot straight away. This will break up the rhythm of your video, and you'll end up reshooting more than you need to.

Shot options

To keep your video interesting, you need some variety! Adjust the camera, film different things in the room or film from different angles. Try this:

Pan and tilt shots – move the camera from left to right (pan) or move the camera up or down (tilt)

pan shot
(left to right)

tilt shot
(up or down)

PRO TIP

While variety is good, moving the camera around too much and adding too many crazy shots can be a bit distracting. You still want your viewers to understand what you're talking about.

Exterior shot – film the location where the video is taking place; if you're filming in a flat, shoot a bit of the outside of the building; exterior shots help your audience to imagine your location

Close-up – get up close and personal to the person, object or place you're filming

Zoom – use the built-in zoom feature to move closer to (zoom in) or further away from (zoom out) the object you're filming; this is sometimes a sliding bar or a button on a digital camera

wide-angle
(pull camera back)

Wide-angle – pull the camera back so that more of the scene is shown

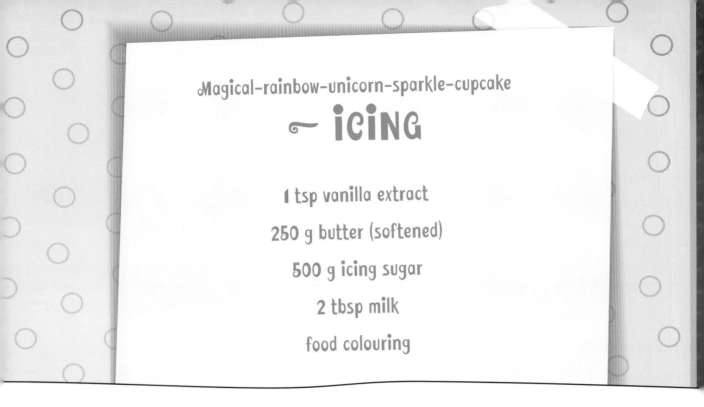

Magical-rainbow-unicorn-sparkle-cupcake ～ ICING

1 tsp vanilla extract

250 g butter (softened)

500 g icing sugar

2 tbsp milk

food colouring

Cutaways

It's always good to get more footage than you need. Did your cat come into the room? Film her! Does your teddy bear have a funny look on its face? Capture it!

PRO TIP

Did you hiccup while filming? Keep it! Throwing that little cutaway in can actually be comedy gold! Learn to laugh at yourself, and your viewers will see you've got a sense of humour.

Cutaways are great ways to give your audience a break. Of course, they'll enjoy watching *you*, but cutting away to something else, even for a second, keeps your vlog fun and interesting. The more cutaways you have to choose from, the happier you'll be when it's time to edit.

33

Playback

You've filmed everything you wanted to talk about. You've been through your entire outline. It's all sitting in your camera, waiting for you to take a look! Grab a notebook and a pencil and watch your footage.

Make notes about what you see. Is there a long pause where nothing is happening? Write that down. Have you missed anything? Remind yourself to film another quick clip to stick in there.

PRO TIP

Ask a friend to look at the footage with you and make notes for edits. Getting a second opinion is always helpful!

PLAYBACK NOTES

1. I stumbled with my wording in the second shot.

2. I forgot to mention a step in making the icing.

3. My voice was too low at the end of the fifth shot.

4. Reshoot the close-ups of the cupcakes.

Editing

OK, now it's time to edit! Editing is like assembling a puzzle. The nice thing about vlogs is that the pieces are usually all shot in order. Putting them together is easy!

Pull all of your video footage into the editing app/software. (Check out page 48 for suggested editing programs.) With your handy editing notes, cut out the pieces you don't want. Add in some of the cutaways you filmed. Consult your outline to make sure everything is in place.

All Clips

Q Search.

Baking with Olivia

0:04 / 0:29

Settings

Reset All

PRO TIP

Never permanently delete the footage you're not using. Hold onto it. You never know when mistakes or alternative shots might come in handy.

Rough cut

The new version of your edited video is what's known as a "rough cut". It has all the pieces put together in the order you want. It should make sense when you watch it from beginning to end.

Play it through and look for other tweaks you can make. The best rule of thumb is to keep it short and sweet. Cut out any coughs, pauses or breaks in the action. Pacing is how well a scene works by keeping things moving. If what's happening on screen seems slow or dull to you, your audience will think so, too. A video with good pacing will keep your audience engaged!

♡ Keep this!

And then jump to a close-up of the sparkles.

☒ Cut some of the mixing time. It's too long.

PRO TIP

Most new video bloggers should try to keep their videos around two minutes or less. It'll be hard to get someone to sit through a video that's 10 to 15 minutes long.

Intro ☆ logo

One thing you'll notice with video bloggers who have been around a while is their intro. An intro is like the opening credits of a TV programme. A video blogger might even have a name for his vlog, such as, "TV Talk with DJ Dustin".

If you decide you want to keep making video blogs, think of a name for it. Consider drawing or making a logo to "brand" your vlog. That will make it stand out from the rest of the video blogs out there. Are you thinking about sharing your video blog on the internet? Ask an adult to help you tag your video and give it a good description. Tagging will help viewers interested in your topic find your vlog.

Let's say your vlog is about TV.
Tag examples:
☆ TV
☆ Reviews
☆ TV Talk with DJ Dustin

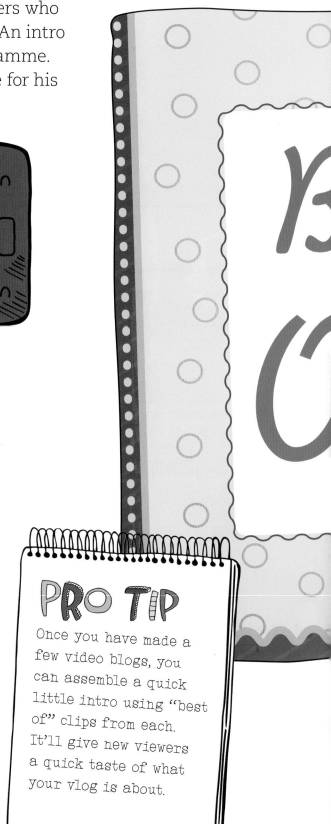

PRO TIP

Once you have made a few video blogs, you can assemble a quick little intro using "best of" clips from each. It'll give new viewers a quick taste of what your vlog is about.

aking with

livia

Music and visual effects

Now that you've edited your video and are happy with it, ask yourself: Is it missing anything else? Consider adding some background music. Music can add another level to your video. Just make sure you don't have the music so loud it drowns out your voice.

Many editing applications have visual effects built in. You can add words that can pop up for emphasis. You can change the video image from colour to black and white. While video effects can be fun, remember that overdoing it can be distracting.

PRO TIP

Make sure you only use music you have permission to use! You can find a lot of "free to use" music on the internet. Just make sure an adult helps you download it.

rainbow-unicorn-sparkle-cupcake
FROSTING

Video blog vanguard!

After all of your great ideas and hard work, your video blog is complete! Now it's time to share it. Have a viewing party so your friends can see what your vlog is all about. Chances are, they'll think it's great and will be hungry for your next one! Do you want to see if people around the world will watch it? Make sure anyone appearing in the video has given you permission to post it.

Then see if your parents/guardians are happy with you uploading it to the internet (YouTube, Vimeo).

Making great video blogs can take some trial and error. With a little practice, finding your voice and style will become as easy as riding a bike. It's fun to become a video blog star. Not only will you be able to share subjects and topics with your friends and family, you might end up finding a larger audience and reaching people all over the world!

PRO TIP

If you don't want to use your real name (or other identifying information), make sure you remove it from the video before posting it online.

Meet your film instructor

Thomas Kingsley Troupe is an amateur filmmaker who has been making films and videos since he was at secondary school. Thomas has worked in the visual effects department for a handful of Hollywood films and shows. He has also written and directed a number of short films for the 48 Hour Film Fest & Z Fest contests and loves creating funny videos with his own sons at home. Thomas says, "Making films is the BEST. It can be a lot of work, but finishing a film to show to your friends and family is WORTH IT!"

Find out more

Books

Behind the Scenes Film Careers (Behind the Glamour),
Danielle S. Hammelef (Raintree, 2018)

Create Your Own Film or TV Show (Media Genius), Matthew Anniss
(Raintree, 2016)

Website

bbc.com/ownit/curations/vlogging
Tips and advice on filming, editing and creating vlogs from top vloggers.

Glossary

app computer application

blog regular feature appearing as part of an online publication that usually relates to a particular topic and consists of articles and personal commentary by one or more authors

consistent always looking or behaving the same

director person who is in charge of a TV programme, film or show

edit cut and rearrange pieces of film to make a film or TV programme

rough cut first version of a film after early editing

script story for a play, film, video blog or TV programme

vanguard forefront of a movement or action

webcam camera used for transmitting live images over the internet

Apps and software

iMovie, by Apple – app to create beautiful movies

Movie Maker Movavi Clips, by Movavi Software, Inc. – advanced video-making app for your smartphone

Movie Maker 10, by Microsoft – full film-making software for all budding artists

Index